Lakota Voices

spoken to

Allen Cody

Cover photos by Edward S. Curtis 1868-1952
Cover design by Cody Allen Taube

Printed in the United States of America
ISBN 978-1-936818-59-4
Library of Congress Control Number: 2021911875

SeaStory Press
1508 Seminary St. #2
Key West. Florida 33040
www.seastorypress.com

Tunkasila watch over us

Sitting Bull

BILL YENNE

"Mitakuye Oyasin" – all life is related.

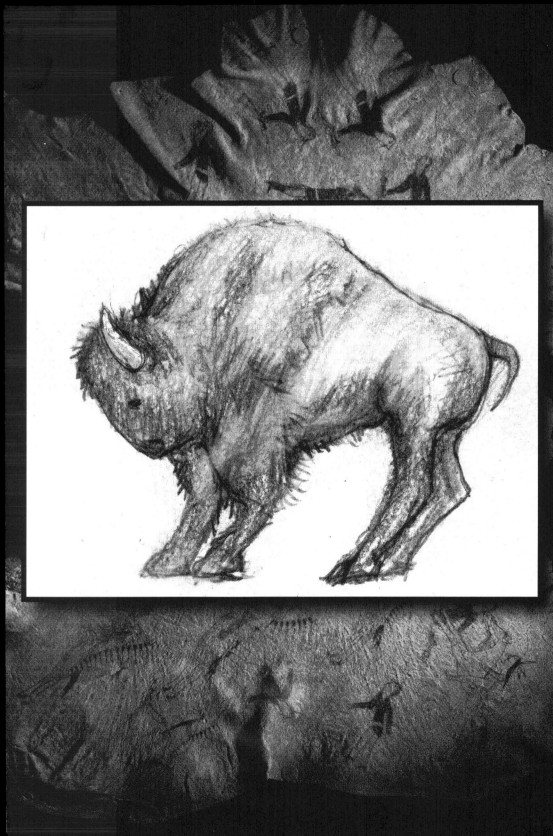

SOUTH DAKOTA – BADLANDS - ERODED PINNACLES OF SANDSTONE

Water rushes under frozen cottonwood-lined river banks

Mighty eagle glides and dives

A mouse stops on a field of snow

Eagle's talons dig in, he lifts the mouse high into the air

Mouse, terrified, looks around as the eagle carries him higher

Mouse knows his life will soon be over, but right now in this most magic time, he is flying through the sky

LAKOTA NARRATOR:

"**I** will tell you a story. It is a story of the Lakota People. It is a story of a brave and wild People who fought valiantly to remain free - but lost the battle.

A once proud People who by losing, lost almost everything. Yes, for a while we lost almost everything - and then they tried to take our Souls and our Spirit.

We have been lying down for a long time. But we are still alive. We are starting to get up now. To taste life again.

Honor and respect for Lakota Chiefs and Warriors who fought hard for the Lakota People

To taste freedom and find and claim our Spirit and our Souls again.

And now more than ever we are desperately trying to move forward to create a good, kind world for our children."

THE BLACK HILLS

WE PEER INTO THE DARK HOLE IN ROCK THAT IS "WIND CAVE"

BRIGHTLY COLORED PRAYER FLAGS, SAGE, SWEETGRASS AND MEDICINE BUNDLES ADORN THE GAPING MOUTH OF THE SMALL CAVE

NARRATOR:

"The elders who can see distant things remember the story of how it began. They say it is how the Lakota People came to be here. The hole that breathes. The Old Ones called this place 'Wind Cave' near Buffalo Gap, in the sacred Black Hills of South Dakota.

QUIET DRUMMING AND SINGING

A cool wind like the shadow of a memory drafts out of the cave from another world.

The Old Ones tell us that Lakota People, our People, crawled from another world, looking for a better one, through the hole in sacred rock.

CHASE IN THE MORNING
SIOUX
Nº 26

Chase in the Morning

First came the buffalo.

BUFFALO CRAWL FROM THE CAVE

KNEELING, THEY STAND, SHAKE THEIR HAIRY BODIES AND
LOOK AROUND AT THIS BRIGHT CLEAR NEW WORLD

Then came the Lakota.

THEY CRAWL OUT AND STAND

THANKFUL WEATHERED INDIAN FACES

TRIBAL SINGING

DRUMS POUND

FACES OF LAKOTA CHILDREN

TIPIS STAND PROUD, PAINTED WITH BEAR, HORSE, DEER
AND BUFFALO

Some say the Spanish Conquistadors, those angry ones,
brought the HORSE. But it was a long time before that
the Horse came to us. We called them 'Sacred Dogs'.

The Horse gave wings to our hunters. 'On horse, we
could shoot twenty arrows in the time it takes to load a
muzzleloader'.

By the 1800s there were many herds of mustangs ranging
wild on the plains.

#26 Rain-in-the-face

Rain in the Face

WILD MUSTANGS STAMPEDE — FLARED NOSTRILS, HOOVES
POUND DIRT, CHOKING DUST RISES

MANY NATIVES RIDE PAINTED HORSES

RIDER AND HORSE — A SINGLE ANIMAL

TRIBAL MUSIC POUNDING

A HUNTER BENDS FORWARD, SHOOTS AN ARROW UNDER
THE NECK OF HIS HORSE

A BUFFALO FALLS

Because horses needed pastures to graze, our encampments were exposed to attack by the Cavalry and by other hostile tribes.

The Horse gave us freedom. Freedom to track herds of wild buffalo. Our camps became mobile. We followed the Buffalo. The Buffalo, Tatanka gave us their lives so the People could live.

From Canada to Mexico the land belonged to us, the creator and no one.

Afraid of Hawk

THE SUNNY PLAINS ROLL BEFORE US

NATIVE ENCAMPMENTS

GIANT HERDS OF BUFFALO STORM THE OPEN PLAINS

FACES OF PROUD SIOUX — STRONG GENTLE AND HUMBLE

NATIVES RIDE PAINTED WAR HORSES

THEY RUSH TOWARD US

A CHIEF RIDES — HE WEARS AN EAGLE FEATHERED
HEADDRESS

TRIBAL MUSIC WAILING

TIPIS ALONG RIVERBANKS

NIGHT SMOKE FROM MANY CAMPFIRES RISES LIKE PRAYER
TO THE STARS

Back then Sioux were made of seven tribes we called the Ocheti Shakowin, Seven Council Fires. The word Lakota means friend or ally. We were connected to, a part of, and we honored Nature.

Nature was sacred and we were all only a small part of Nature and of Life.

But white settlers were moving west. They wanted our Land.

Looking Horse

Tired of fighting many battles, we signed The Fort Laramie Treaty of 1851 that gave us the Great Plains 'as long as the river flows and the eagle flies."

A WEATHERED YELLOW PARCHMENT

FORT LARAMIE TREATY UNROLLS BEFORE US

In trade we granted white settlers and gold miners freedom to transit the Oregon Trail.

The U.S. Cavalry then attacked a peaceful village and killed one hundred men, women and children.

DISPLACED NATIVES

CRYING CHILDREN

SLOW SAD TRIBAL MUSIC

NATIVE CAMPS ON FIRE

TIPIS BURN—FIRES CRACKLE

While we fought for our lives, treaties were broken and our ancestor's homeland was gobbled up by the U.S. federal government.

Young Man Afraid of His Horses

(They Fear His Horses)

WAR CHANTS AND DRUMS

PRISTINE RAW WILDERNESS

BEAVER, BEAR, DEER,

FORESTS, RUSHING STREAMS —

THE WILD BLACK HILLS OF SOUTH DAKOTA

In the Second Laramie Treaty of 1868 the Sioux agreed to trade millions of acres of prairie for Paha Sapa, the most sacred Black Hills, which were deeded to us 'forever, so long as the buffalo may range thereupon…'."

WILL:
"We assumed we were dealing with honorable people."

NARRATOR:
"The government's promise of 'forever' lasted only four years, until the day White Men discovered gold in the Black Hills."

Red Horse

CREAKING COVERED WAGONS WITH WHITE SETTLERS
CRAWL WESTWARD

RAILROADS, MINES, FORTS

WHITE WOODEN CHURCHES SPROUT

TOWNS GROW LIKE ACNE ON THE RUGGED FACE OF THE
WILDERNESS

GENERAL WM. TECUMSEH SHERMAN:

"The more Indians we can kill this year, the less will have to be killed in the next war, for the more I see of these Indians, the more convinced I am that they all have to be killed or be maintained as a species of paupers."

NARRATOR:

"President Ulysses S Grant sent an ambitious young soldier to deal with 'The Indian Problem'.

That soldier was someone who had his own claim to gold mining rights in The Black Hills - a Bluecoat the Lakota call - 'Yellow Hair Fool'- George Armstrong Custer.

15

Sitting Bull
& nephew, One Bull

LEUTENANT COLONEL GEORGE ARMSTRONG CUSTER ON HIS
    WHITE HORSE

LONGER WAGON TRAINS

TRIBAL MUSIC SCREECHING

FORTS

SIOUX ENCAMPMENTS

When Sitting Bull learned of Grant's plan, he called a council of all the great tribes of the plains.

SMOKE SIGNALS

LOUD DRUMMING

ULYSSES GRANT'S SOLDIERS MARCH

U.S. 7TH CAVALRY ON HORSEBACK

SIOUX ENCAMPMENTS

NATIVE WARIORS ON HORSEBACK AS FAR AS THE EYE CAN
    SEE

Thousands of warriors journeyed to the camp of Sitting Bull. Never before and never again so many Indians from so many nations gathered to unite together: The Sioux. The Cheyenne. The Crow. The Arapaho. The Blackfoot.

82572

Chief Gall

WAR HORSES PAINTED WITH HANDS, HAIL STONES, ARROWS, LIGHTNING BOLTS

DRUMS BEAT

NATIVE WOMEN TRILL

MANY FIERCE WAR-PAINTED WARRIOR BROTHERS RIDE TOGETHER

The warriors sundanced and prayed to the Creator. They sang songs of war. And listened to the words of Sitting Bull."

SITTING BULL:

"The sacred land belongs to us! If the outsiders try to take it, we will fight! Join with me, brothers. Walk the Red Road for the Creator and for our children.

Wakan Tankan, pity me, in the name of the People I offer the sacred pipe to you. Wherever the sun, the moon, the earth, the four points of wind, there you are always. Save the People I beg of you – we want to live. Pity me. I am Sitting Bull."

NARRATOR:

"The Tribes fought the Blue Coats who had betrayed their trust once more."

Chief Corn

Natives and blue coats entwined in battle

Smoke and the percussion of rifle and of cannon

Custer, shot with many arrows falls off his white horse

The raging battle of little big horn

WEBSTER:

"General Sheridan called us the greatest light Calvary ever to live on the face of the earth."

Smoke

Noise of battle

Natives swing war axes, shoot arrows

Natives fire Henry and Winchester rifles

The great American seventh cavalry falls

NARRATOR:

"Our Indian forces outnumbered Custer's, but in his ambition to defeat Sitting Bull, he led his men right into the battle. And at the Battle of Little Big Horn, we call Greasy Grass Creek, our Indians annihilated the white soldiers.

Crazy Horse rode his war horse right into the enemy.

Chief Crazy Horse

They fired their rifles at him many times, but none of their bullets could bring him down."

CRAZY HORSE RIDES

CAVALRY SHOOTS MANY ROUNDS AT HIM

SOUNDS OF BATTLE

CANNONS BOOM AND RUMBLE

LIGHT FLASHES FROM KNIVES, HATCHETS AND SWORDS

RIFLES FIRE

HORSES CHARGE

SMOKE AND DUST RISE

CRAZY HORSE:
"HOKAHEY!" It is a good day to die, follow me!"

BATTLE OF LITTLE BIG HORN

NARRATOR:
"After the great battle, General Alfred Terry traveled north to offer Sitting Bull full pardon on condition he and his men move back on the reservation."

Chief Flying Hawk

SITTING BULL TALKS TO GENERAL TERRY – BOTH ON HORSEBACK

SITTING BULL TALKS TO GENERAL TERRY – BOTH ON HORSEBACK

SITTING BULL:

"This country is my country and I intend to stay here and raise my People to fill it. We did not give our country to you; you stole it. You come here to tell lies; when you go home, take your lies with you."

Flying Hawk, Oglala Lakota 1854-1931 tells of the Indian Wars.

FLYING HAWK:

When the great Sioux war came, we had lots of battles with the soldiers. We were fighting all the time with Miles and Crook and white soldiers every place we went.

I was not in the fight at Wounded Knee, but was there right after the soldiers shot our women and children with machine guns and killed so many. The soldiers were wrong. They treated us bad. The army of the white people were afraid of us.

They did not like Red Cloud because he talked and told the truth about dishonest agents. They put him in the guard-house at Fort Robinson and put a stick in his mouth (indicating three inches) and tied his hands so he could not talk when the army officers came to inspect.

Sitting Bull was all right but they got afraid of him and killed him.

Little Big Man

They were afraid of my cousin, Crazy Horse, so they killed him. These were acts of cowards. It was murder. We were starving. We only wanted food.

Crazy Horse was my cousin and best friend. A soldier ran a bayonet through his back. He was unarmed and two other men held him by the arms when the white soldier came up behind him and put his bayonet through his kidney.

I got there a few minutes after he was stabbed.

When he was dead, his father and brothers took him away and buried him. They never told where he is buried and now, we do not know.

Crazy Horse was never with other Indians unless it was in a fight. He was always the first in a fight and the soldiers could not beat him in a fight. He won every fight with the whites.

The young brother of Crazy Horse was on a trip where now is Utah and there he was killed by some white settlers. They were having some trouble with the Indians there.

When Crazy Horse learned that his brother was killed, he took his wife with him and went away, but told no one where he was going. He was gone for a long time.

He went to the place where his brother was killed and camped in the woods where he could see the settlement. He stayed there nine days. Every day he would look

Touch the Clouds

around and when he saw someone, he would shoot him. He killed enough to satisfy and then came home.

Crazy Horse married but had no children. He was much alone. He never told stories and never took a scalp from his enemies when he killed them.

He was the bravest chief we ever had. He was the leader and the first and front in the Custer fight.

He never talked but always acted first. He was my friend and we went in the Custer fight together."

NARRATOR:
"Greasy Grass Ridge was to be our last victory. The larger struggle would last until forever."

GENERAL SHERIDAN:
"We must kill the buffalo as a means of destroying the Indians..."

BUFFALO GRAZE ON THE GRASSY PLAINS

NARRATOR:
"And they did. The Whites slaughtered sixty million buffalo.

M-4 Chief Charlo and Grandaughter, Western Montana

Chief Charlo & Grandaughter

The Cattlemen's Association traveled to Washington D.C., to lobby and bribe U.S Senators.

With huge herds of buffalo free for the taking, their cattle were worthless, and the nuisance Indians were always in the way - so a bounty was placed on buffalo skulls and on Indian scalps and they were both killed for fun and profit.

In 1873 one and a half million buffalo were slaughtered.

By 1893 there were estimated only 300 living buffalo left in the entire country. Our four-footed brother upon whom we depended for food, shelter, clothing and medicine had disappeared.

The drumming of their hooves had kept the water table close to the surface while the buffalo fertilized the great green prairie.

When all the buffalo were gone, the prairie became dustbowl and the white farmers had to abandon the land stolen from the Indians.

A BUFFALO HUNTER SMIRKS, HOLDS HIS RIFLE AND POSES ON TOP OF A 3-STORY PILE OF BUFFALO SKULLS

WEATHERED FACES OF OLD INDIANS

LEON:
"The world knows what happened to us. Problem is, the victor always writes the history books."

Little Horse

WILL:
"They gave us blankets infested with small pox. We barely survived our own holocaust. We barely survived our own genocide."

HAROLD:
"Then Jesuits were sent in to try to stop the traditional practice of Lakota medicine and prayer. They would take certain Indian people and use them to find out where the ceremonies were taking place."

OLD CHURCH AT FORT RANDALL

MADONNA THUNDER HAWK:
"It was a survival mechanism for our people. It wasn't so much 'what Christian church do you belong to?' it was 'just please keep the missionaries away'…"

COURTHOUSE, KYLE, S. DAKOTA

RAE ANN, Associate Judge, Lakota Nation:
"There was a whole era where children were forced into boarding schools, they literally had the language beat out of them."

the Children

34

CARLISLE INDIAN INDUSTRIAL SCHOOL, CARLISLE PENNSYLVANIA

Jesuit boarding schools

Nuns in habits swing two-by-fours

Priests weild straps

Native children cry

RAE ANN:
"Grandma spoke fluently as a child and got whipped for speaking it."

PINE RIDGE TRIBAL ASSISTANCE TRAILER

LYLE: Psychotherapist (60s)
"I had to go to an Indian boarding school when I was young. They cut our hair off and we all wore the same kind of uniform, kind of military. Some general in the army, name of Pratt, he had that idea. The way to assimilate Native Americans was similar to military tactics. So we marched, we had a place to stand, roll call, and we had to do calisthenics in the morning. We marched to church, we marched to school, we marched to the mess hall. We were always marched."

Chief Whirlwind Soldier

REZ HOUSE AT ROSEBUD

IRENE:

"At one time we were punished. I refused to speak English. I'm glad I still speak my language."

PHYLLIS:

"We had three generations of boarding schools that broke the bond of mother-child-grandchild."

TRIBAL MENTAL HEALTH OFFICE

LYLE:

"They beat us to death with two-by-fours for disciplinary actions. I caught it on the behind with a two-by-eight many times. We got knocked down many times."

FACES OF SAD NATIVE CHILDREN

NARRATOR:

"Under the Indian Civilization Act and the Indian Boarding School Policy our children were rounded up like cattle for slaughter, torn away from their families and taken to Christian and government boarding schools far away from their homelands and families.

In 1900 there were 20,000 children in Indian boarding schools where the Indian was beat, starved and tortured out of these little children, while they were forced to

Brave Buffalo

forsake language and tradition.

Their traditional clothing was burned, their long hair cut. By 1925 60,889, that is 83% of Indian children, were attending more than 357 boarding schools in 30 states.

Many were never returned to their families and simply disappeared.

Those who could not conform were called 'Untamed Savages'. There were graveyards behind each boarding school for the broken bodies of children who failed to become obedient little white people.

Many Natives of many countries today bear the scars of this inhumanity.

WHITE WOOD CROSSES BEHIND AN INDIAN SCHOOL

SUN DANCERS PRAY

THEY BLOW EAGLE BONE WHISTLES WHILE PIERCED AND
TETHERED TO A SACRED COTTONWOOD TREE

The 1883 Statute banned our most important spiritual ceremony—Sun Dance.

In some Indian families Sun Dance, Lakota language, and our traditional ways went on in secret to keep alive what little remained of our spirit and Lakota culture."

Chief Red Cloud

THOMPSEN'S FARM

JAMES:

"This was all taken underground, outlawed, we were told not to do this. The old ones took ceremonies underground. The government sent spies to watch that the crazy Indians don't go crazy..."

CHIEF RED CLOUD

NARRATOR:

"Red Cloud said: 'The white man broke every promise he ever made, except one. He promised to take our land... and he did.'

Between 1890 and 1910 the total Indian population fell to less than 250,000 from over 4,000,000 in 1492. The American Indian was nearly facing extinction.

NATIVE PEOPLE, SICK AND STARVING

The great herds of buffalo were disappearing. We had two options: sign another treaty which would force us onto reservations -- or face starvation.

The treaty promised food, shelter, education and medical help for us and our descendants for 'forever'."

Iron White Man

CHIEF IRON WHITE MAN

HOUSE AT ROSEBUD

IRENE (56, looking 80) sits at her kitchen table, smoking a hand-rolled cigarette:
"I don't know what I can say. I believe in my treaty rights, I should get what I'm due."

AGAY (50s) Educator and Tribal Leader:
"These are not hand-outs, these are what are owed to us from our treaties. It's what our forefathers signed when they put their thumbprints on those treaties so our People would be protected, they'd have the health and the housing and the shelter and the security. All of our tribes in the great plains are treaty tribes. As such, our People always stand on the treaties. That's why to us it's so important."

WILL:
"Maybe it's time America comes clean with its promises. How can we expect other countries to enter into treaties with us when America can't keep the promises it made within our own country?"

Joseph Two Bulls

Rᴇᴢ ᴅᴏɢꜱ ʟᴏᴜɴɢᴇ ᴜɴᴅᴇʀ ᴛʜᴇ ꜱᴀᴅ ꜱᴛʀᴜᴄᴛᴜʀᴇ ᴇᴠᴇɴ
    ᴛʜᴏᴜɢʜ ɪᴛ'ꜱ ᴍɪɴᴜꜱ **35** ᴅᴇɢʀᴇᴇꜱ

Tᴀᴛᴛᴇʀᴇᴅ ᴀᴍᴇʀɪᴄᴀɴ ꜰʟᴀɢ ꜰʟᴀᴘꜱ

Aɴᴏᴛʜᴇʀ ʜᴏᴜꜱᴇ

Aᴍᴇʀɪᴄᴀɴ ꜰʟᴀɢ ᴜᴘꜱɪᴅᴇ–ᴅᴏᴡɴ

NARRATOR:

"From 1641 until 1911 there were government-paid bounties offered for men, women and children Indian scalps.

In 1862 President Lincoln ordered the biggest mass execution in US history – they hanged thirty-eight Dakota Indians in Mankato, Minnesota.

It wasn't until 1928 our captors grudgingly allowed the original North American Natives to become American citizens.

The BIA (Bureau of Indian Affairs) practiced secret forced sterilization of Native American women until mid 1970s.

It wasn't until May 19, 2005 that Massachusetts repealed a law that made it illegal for an Indian to enter Boston.

In 1952 the Tekakwitha Indian Mission could sell you a Native Child, boy or girl for $10.00."

Six Grandfathers

Sundancers pray

PHYLLIS:

"Sundance was prohibited for sixty years. So, only in 1978 were we granted the freedom of religion by an act of Congress."

NARRATOR:

"The sad truth is that what the Lakota lost of their rich culture may never be regained.

Mount Rushmore is eighty-two miles from the Pine Ridge Lakota Reservation in the Black Hills.

Mount Rushmore was called The Six Grandfathers in the Sacred Black Hills before they carved the faces of the white American Presidents, each of them had oppressed, slaughtered and removed the Native Americans from their land.

After gold was discovered in the Black Hills, the Government seized The Six Grandfathers and President Grant secretly commanded his generals not to protect local Indian tribes while bounty hunters collected $300 for an Indian scalp.

In 1927 sculptor Gutxon Borglum, a white supremist and dedicated follower of the Ku Klux Klan, began to plan out and carve the four faces, George Washington, Thomas Jefferson, Abraham Lincoln and Theodore Roosevelt in granite, a project funded mostly by the KKK."

Russell Means

COURTHOUSE, KYLE SOUTH DAKOTA

RAE:

"When our People were put on reservations, they took away the man's role in providing for his family. Our men were highly honored, respected, esteemed. They were warriors. Never a question about providing and protecting. Now there is nothing for them to do. Indian agents would undermine men, went against who we were as a People. The role of women is intact. When you have a man stripped of his abilities... it's devastating."

RUSSELL MEANS, NATIVE ACTIVIST, AUTHOR AND ACTOR

BRIGHT TURQUOISE, SILVER JEWELRY,

LONG BRAIDS WRAPPED IN LEATHER

RUSSELL MEANS:

"The men have been so debilitated; they have extremely low self-esteem."

HIGHER GROUNDS COFFEE HOUSE

LEON:

"The reservations are concentration camps. They've tried to destroy a whole People group. We have a tragic history.

Spotted Eagle

We are the remnants of a once-great People. Our society wasn't perfect, but it worked..."

RUSSELL MEANS:

"Listen. The statistics of deprivation that we suffered under the colonial apartheid system were safely tucked away out of sight, out of mind. The colonial apartheid system of the Indian Policies of America is exterminating us. We're within ten to fifteen years of extermination."

WILL:

"I guess it's for us, just like it was for our ancestors. We're less than human. That's why it's okay just to wipe us out, throw the remains in a big old giant hole."

WILL:

"Reflections of what happened to the Jewish people. Hitler loved cowboy movies, Ma said he got his ideals of oppression and all this stuff from what United States did to Native Americans."

Eagle Staff

RAPID CITY, S. DAKOTA

DOWNTOWN

CARS

CLEAN STREETS

STOREFRONTS

ART GALLERIES

GOVERNMENT OFFICES

MAYOR'S OFFICE

MAYOR ALAN HANKS:

"In my position as mayor I can't go back and change things that happened 200 years ago or 100 years or even 50 years ago. All too often when we talk about racism they want to talk about the past. It's not that it's not important to them, but we can't do anything about it on the local level. We can talk about it but we need to move forward. Look at the past but be dedicated to move into the future."

Big Foot (also called Spotted Elk)

WILL'S LIVING ROOM

SUNGLASSES COVER HIS EYES

ABALONE SHELL EARRINGS DANGLE FROM HIS EAR LOBES

WILL IS AN INTENSE LAKOTA IN HIS 40S

HE SITS ON THE EDGE OF A LEATHER SOFA

WILL:

"Let me come to your house, man, with my relatives. Let us rampage through your house, rape your women and kill your children and kill your old people and steal everything from you.

A month from now, we'll say hey, that happened in the past, forget about it, you gotta move on. I'll grab your grandchild throw him up in the air and I'll shoot his head. I'll grab his ankles and I'll bash his head on the counter like they did to the People in 1890 at Wounded Knee.

AFTERMATH OF MASSACRE AT WOUNDED KNEE — BODIES OF MEN, WOMEN AND BABIES FROZEN INTO THE SNOW

High Horse

Two months from now, when you still try to get somebody to arrest me I'll say, hey that happened in the past, forget about it, man. You know, let it go.

I'll destroy your home. And in the American judicial system, I should pay for that. But I ain't gonna pay jack, man.

You take me to court and I'll get on the stand and say hey let it go, that happened in the past, get over it."

TOM DASCHLE (former South Dakota Senator):

"...our country put them on the absolute worst land, the least productive land anywhere to be found and that's why they're there. They were put there because no non-Indians wanted to go there. We relegated them to the poorest land and then we say 'we can't figure out why you can't do anything.'"

PINE RIDGE

SCRUFFY DOGS

STRIPPED CARS

BROKEN HOUSES

Gassy (I-api-otah)

NARRATOR:

"Sioux live in reservation conditions equal to the most poverty-stricken third world country. Average life expectancy of Lakota men is forty-nine years. Rates of teen suicide, tuberculosis and cervical cancer, off the charts. Infant mortality, alcoholism, drug abuse, spousal abuse, racism, crimes against native women and girls and their disappearance ravages our community."

SOUTH DAKOTA STATE UNIVERSITY

RUSS:

"It's sad, but then again you gotta think. If you're fifteen years old, what do you have to look forward to?

Your dad might be in prison, your mom hasn't come home and if she does come home, she might bring a boyfriend. The last time you got beat up. We've heard these stories. So, what's the point? And then somebody shows up saying 'Go to college!' And you have no clue even how to get through high school."

ROSEBUD RESERVATION

A NEW PICKUP TRUCK STOPS AT RUN-DOWN RESERVATION TRAILER

James, medicine man, climbs out of his truck. He knocks on the door, it cracks open. He speaks to someone, then walks back to the truck.

High Bear
(Mato Wakantuya)

TRUCK — MOVING

JAMES:

"Two little kids home. Their mom's in jail, their dad just went to town with his check. Probably buying booze. Why aren't these kids in school?"

WINTER

SNOW, ROCKS, TREES, SKY

WE ARE SURROUNDED BY SNOW AND ICE

TRIBAL SINGING

PINE RIDGE HOUSING DEVELOPMENT

MORE RUN-DOWN HOUSES

TRAILERS ON CINDER BLOCKS

BOB:

"I don't know if you've ever spent a South Dakota winter, but the temperature can get to 30 below zero with a -30-degree wind chill factor and 100 below zero wind chill is not uncommon.

When you get out to the reservation and see these little old houses and just imagine, sometimes there are three

Crazy Walking

or four families living in there, living on a gramma's paycheck. And the kids have never slept on a mattress, they've always slept on the floor.

GARBAGE BLOWS DOWN THE STREET

SKINNY, STARVING PACKS OF REZ DOGS, NOSES TO THE GROUND, SEARCH THE STREETS FOR SCRAPS OF FOOD

ONE DOG LICKS A SMUDGE ON THE ROAD

WILL:

"Indigenous people, we're living in man-made disaster areas. Not natural disasters like what happened to the poor folks the victims of Katrina. These are man-made disaster areas."

RUSS:

"On the rez, the average housing occupancy is seventeen people per home. Toxic mold is killing us.

There's nothing out there. Unemployment is 85%. Maybe what we've been told is false. Maybe every Indian doesn't have a Cadillac. Maybe we have suicide rates that are astronomical."

MARK:

"People here don't own the land under their houses, it's

Sammy Lone Bear

held in trust by the federal government. And so, investing in a home, buying and selling a home is not a possibility here at all."

IRENE'S HOUSE AT ROSEBUD

Two little girls watch television from an unmade bed. One of them cradles a cat like a baby. Wind blows through the cracks.

WHITE RIVER BANK – James stands outside a sweat lodge.

TRIBAL SINGING

DRUMMING

JAMES:
"These trees could tell stories... they have seen it all. Sitting Bull camped right there. (James points to cottonwood trees along the White River) Sitting Bull was our main visionary. He was a man of power. He was a man of wisdom. He was a man of sight."

CLINT:
"The People we looked up to were Sitting Bull, Crazy Horse and Red Cloud. Where are the People today for kids to look up to?"

Hollow Horn Bear

HAROLD'S CEREMONY ROOM

SUNDANCE ARTIFACTS

WARBONETS

BEADED PIPE CASES

EAGLE FEATHERS

OTHER CEREMONIAL GEAR

HAROLD:

"The cause has lived on, him and Crazy Horse. The cause is what's here in Lakota culture today. They're dying for what they believed in, so when you get involved in Lakota ceremony or anything to do with Lakota things, they're the ones you hear about."

SWEAT LODGE

NARRATOR:

"When you go in the sweat lodge to cleanse, to pray - they're in there with you. In there in the dark. In the heat. In the sweat. In there with the Stone People, with your friends, your family, the old ones, ancestors, Sitting Bull,

Jack Red Cloud

Crazy Horse, Red Cloud. All of Them. They're with us in there, with us in the dark, listening to our prayer. They are praying with us that our People will live..."

PINE RIDGE HIGH SCHOOL

RAP MUSIC PLAYS

INDIAN TEENS SMOKE CIGARETTES — DRINK WHISKY — SNORT COKE — SHOOT DRUGS INTO THEIR VEINS

CLINT:

"I see posters of Tupac and all these other big rock stars, and they idolize them, they sit there singing their songs, dressing like them, talking like them."

RUSSELL MEANS:

"Here's the reason why: it doesn't pay to be an Indian. They look around, see their parents, see how they're treated. And they see pow wow people all dressed up in feathers, but that doesn't pay. It pays to be a rapper, hip hop, but it doesn't pay to be an Indian."

KILI RADIO STATION

ARLO:

"We can work on drugs and alcohol all we want but without cultural identity, something else is going to snap our kids up."

Luther Standing Bear

HIGHER GROUNDS COFFEE SHOP

LISA (14):

"There's not that much to do, so they join gangs, nothing else to do, to be cool. There's cocaine all the time. Most everybody drinks a lot too. My little brother's in a gang. He's ten."

BOWLING ALLEY

MARCY:

"Oh, you can see it, the ones that have chips on their shoulder, even the little kids, so upset, so negative, five and eight years old..."

LYLE:

"There's a breakdown of the culture."

PRAIRIE EDGE GALLERY

CLINT:

"My father died when I was nine. I went to live with my mother in Montana who was living with another man and she eventually got married to him and had another child from him. But she had issues to deal with too, so I ended up in boarding school in Montana until she decided not to be with the man she was with anymore.

Blue Horse

AMERICAN INDIAN MOVEMENT (A.I.M) FLAG RIPPLES IN THE BREEZE

MEMBERS RAISE THEIR FISTS OUT THE WINDOWS AS REZ RUNNERS SPEED BY ON DIRT ROADS

And she was running around with AIM back then too. She was in that crowd too. When I got to finally know her a little bit, because she left us when I was five, me and my little brother and I never really knew until I was ten. That seemed to be the deal with her, if she was dealing with stuff I don't know.

But I got introduced to drugs and alcohol then. It was just a normal thing, jump in, be part of the boys."

SCHOOL ON THE RESERVATION

GRAFFITTI ON WALLS

TRASH BLOWS ON PLAYGROUND

WILL:

"I was on the tribal council on the judiciary committee. Meth was starting to come into our community. We already got everything else, we got crack, coke, weed.

Little Wound

A big drug ring went down, a convenient drug ring, a drug ring of people who weren't politically connected. But the moment they were taken out of the picture, they were replaced.

We wanted our police force to do something about it, man. We wanted our police force to start kicking in doors, probable cause, man, you know. A lot of people go into somebody's house and walk away with a baggie of drugs, man, that's probable cause. Kick in the door, start busting people.

The ones who stopped it, who even threatened our good police officers, were the Feds. The Feds said, 'You're obstructing justice, you're obstructing an investigation. We're going after the big top guys at the head of these drug things and so you guys need to not be busting the small-time dealers and all that because we want to get the big guys.'

So, what does that mean? In the meantime we got to pay the price, so you could get the big guy? And the human toll means nothing? We got to see generations of our children's talents being squandered on these small-time drug dealers who are selling them this stuff.

You know I've seen this runner who was a state champion have that all taken away from him because he got hooked on drugs. I've seen children just at the very edge of their potential, ready to go on to college, ready to do this and that. And it's gone. You know, we've seen Young People, their very lives snuffed out of them."

Medicine Cloud

GYMNASIUM – RED CLOUD HIGH SCHOOL

BASKETBALL PLAYERS RUN DOWN THE COURT

HIGH SCHOOL ROOM

LESTER, BILLY, MIKE AND ARTHUR

MIKE:

"Never had a steady home... my mom's an alcoholic, my dad left when I was three."

ARTHUR (16):

"I grew up in Wounded Knee. I see all the drugs and alcohol and want something better."

BILL:

"Alcoholism has been a terrible thing for them and drugs now, and certainly you have seventy or eighty percent unemployment on the rez, and not much hope for the Young People, it's got to be terrible."

CLINT:

"White people have more experience with alcohol, Indians can't handle it. You just basically stay stuck. There's no hope. So they turn to dope, to alcohol. They take what little money they earn and use it on drugs and alcohol."

RUSS:

"There is alcoholism. They go right across the border and there's a guy in Nebraska selling it."

WHITE CLAY, NEBRASKA

A tiny town of many liquor stores

RUSSELL MEANS:

"Their welfare money doesn't even hit their pocket. It goes straight to the White Man and his liquor stores."

JAMES:

"Alcohol is something you get into by making a multitude of wrong choices. We call them diseases so you can blame it on the disease."

CLINT:

"Alcoholism gets worse and pretty soon they're no more."

DEB:

"The use of alcohol and drugs. It's just overturned our reservations. Many women as well as men do have that problem. And that is very sad. Because we're a nation and we are losing everything what we were taught."

CLINT:

"I've been in a lot of trouble over it, legal trouble and stuff. It's become a way of life on the reservation. It's been that way for years."

Lost Medicine

BRAVE NATIVE WARRIORS RIDING WAR HORSES

HAROLD:

"Alcohol allowed them to be Indian. They could feel Lakota again, being under the influence of alcohol. Indians, when they drink, they just have fun. To them that's fun. They just don't know when to stop. They literally died like flies because of alcohol."

DESERTED POW-WOW GROUNDS

STEAMING SWEAT LODGE

CLINT:

"I had problems with drugs and alcohol. But after I got time to sit with medicine men and pipe carriers and singers and stuff and brought back into this way of life, it gave me an opportunity to take a look at all that stuff.

Sitting in a sweat lodge and they tell me to leave it all there, just leave it. It's basically just a purification ceremony. You go in there to pray, clean your heart and your mind. Through traditional songs and prayer and… the rocks."

Iron Tail

RAPID CITY

CAR DEALERSHIPS

WALMART PACKED WITH REZ NATIVES

MARK:

"If you notice where the big stores are in Rapid City and border town car dealerships, they're all on the roads that come in from the reservations.

I believe there's a tacit conspiracy of all the border town banks and commercial interests to keep anything from happening here because all the federal dollars and all the private foundation money, everything that comes into the reservation flows out instantly to off-reservation vendors, dealers, cars, movie theaters. It's been that way for a hundred and forty years and as far as the border towns are concerned, it can stay that way for another hundred and forty years.

How could you have an area the size of Connecticut in the United States of America without a bank unless there was a conspiracy? Tacit conspiracy to keep the reservation poor.

And it has to do with the fact that since the reservation was founded, the Indian People had to take their wagons and trade off the reservation to get the things they needed to survive - from oil for their lamps to clothing to shoes to parts for their wagons to farming implements.

Moving Robe Woman
fought against Custer at Greasy Grass,
to avenge her brother, One Hawk

That relationship between the reservations and the border towns is unchanged for over a hundred and forty years. So that every dollar that flows into the reservation within 24 hours of payday and often within an hour or two hours of the check landing in the hand of the Native employee, it's in a border town being spent on groceries, haircuts, cars, everything. All the services you can imagine. And so therefore, we don't have an internal economy.

So the opportunity for Young Lakota People to have a job, to get their first job, to earn a paycheck, to feel good about themselves and support their family is very very frustrated and very difficult.

The banks will argue, they'll say, well, the tribal government is not stable. The tribe doesn't have a UCC, a Uniform Commercial Code, they'll come up with one excuse after another. And as the tribe eliminates those excuses, such as having a Uniform Commercial Code, the day that a bank will arrive here comes no quicker."

BOWLING ALLEY

MARCY (non-Native):
"You know, Native Americans got the world by the tail if they'd take it."

Clear

SMALL TRIBAL CASINO

NARRATOR:

"The Whiteman thinks we're getting rich off our casinos."

WILL:

"We use our casino profits if there are any to supplement for elderly programs and tribal programs and youth programs. We're not gonna get rich off gaming, we're just gonna survive."

PINE RIDGE, A HOME FOR ELDERLY

Lakota caregivers wheelchair residents into a building

FORT RANDALL CASINO

IZZY:

"We've had this here casino fifteen years, the first fourteen we couldn't get financial statements from these people. Everything's backwards. It's all nepotism here."

HIGHER GROUNDS COFFEE SHOP

LEON:

"There's so much death here. That brings on a lot of the alcoholism, the drug abuse. People medicate themselves.

Fool Thunder
& family

And we deal with historical trauma, the aftermath of having a way of life taken away. Take away the food source, kill the buffalo."

WILL:

"When you bury all kinds of Young People, man. The first one was way too much, you know. When you see things that were meant for your People being taken away without even somebody saying 'hey, wait a minute we should go to court over this here stuff, man.' We have a legally binding contract here, you know. But you don't have enough, it's kind of sad, I don't think there's enough of us to form a good war party anymore. I don't know what it's gonna take."

MENTAL HEALTH OFFICE

LYLE:

"A long time ago our ancestors said, suicide came in a dark form. It's here. It effects the minds of our Native Americans. Fifteen to twenty-four years of age for Native Americans. That fluctuates but that's the age. There are many reasons - poverty, unemployment, relational issues, health-wise, sicknesses, the historic trauma is still active here, how the government mistreated our Native Americans passed down from generation to generation."

Painted Horse

PHOTOGRAPHER'S STUDIO

BILL (85), PHOTOGRAPHER STANDS IN FRONT OF A
PORTRAIT OF A LAKOTA CHIEF IN FULL HEADDRESS.

BILL:
"They think they have it tough, and they do."

WILL:
"Things happen here that violate not only the Major Crimes Act, but warrant Federal investigations and Federal action. But when it comes to things happening with tribes, the Feds are like, 'Oh we don't want to interfere with your sovereignty.' And that's just a cop out man, just a cop out.

They might as well say, 'Oh we'd prefer it if you just all killed each other and get yourselves out of the way of us.' I have seen unsolved murders here. We have two back there, close to being decapitated, man. Just a little over a year ago, a young man was stabbed to death. You never know how People die around here, you find them dead somewhere behind a business or in a ditch. You don't know if it's self-inflicted like alcohol poisoning or drug overdose. When babies die you don't know how they die, when women die, when old people die.

I tell you, there's an element here, I think poor people, the kind of people that everybody likes to walk on top of, they ignore, act like they're better than, it's all bullshit

Little Hawk

man, there's nothing that you can have in this world that makes you better than other people.

They're human beings too. But to try to get something done about it, man.

I remember dealing with a family who had a son that a policeman cuffed him so tight that they messed up his circulatory system in one hand, that hand was becoming dead so they had to cut it off. When I went to go talk to this young guy, man he was really skittish, man. And he had a great spirit of fear in him, man.

Even in my own family, there's been attacks, brutal attacks that leave a lifetime injury. And we're standing up on the highest hill yelling for help, man. 'Hey we've been attacked here!' And there's mothers out there still out there saying, 'Bring justice for my son, we know who killed him'."

OFFICE

RUSSELL MEANS:
"At AIM after Wounded Knee, sixty-two AIM sympathizers were killed and it was never investigated. Lately two people killed in White Clay, Nebraska. And they were found, their bodies tossed in a ditch."

Walter Iron Shell

WILL:

"There's always a reason why somebody can't do something. And the cases I've been involved in I've been from the top of the mountain and stopped at every little place in-between, asking, 'Send somebody over to investigate this,' you know. The only times they want to do investigations is with really heavy-duty court action is to shut People up like me, and to shut that Mama up and to shut that Gramma up too. Victims of crime get re-victimized by corrupt elements of a corrupt police force."

RAPID CREEK, RAPID CITY

RUSSELL MEANS:

"There was a serial killer about ten years ago in Rapid City who was killing homeless Indians and they'd always find the body in Rapid Creek.

NEWSPAPER — LAST PAGE

SMALL ARTICLE ABOUT AN INDIAN MURDER

About five or six Indians within a year and a half, and then all of a sudden, he quit. No one was ever charged or found out, and we don't know if the police ever investigated."

Running Antelope

MAYOR'S OFFICE

MAYOR ALAN HANKS:

"The perception is that there is no hope for a better life in the future. The first thing we need to do to address the issue in terms of education and racism."

SOUTH DAKOTA STATE UNIVERSITY

RUSS:

"It's downstream upstream thinking. Are you going to wait until they get in trouble downstream or are you gonna educate them upstream? To keep them out of the prison. I mean, it's that simple."

MADONNA:

"We are still a tribal People, our bodies are still back in the time of hunting and gathering, the bodies of an Indian Person cannot handle a modern-day diet. It's killing us with diabetes and heart trouble."

COMMODITIES OUTLET

NARRATOR:

"Government food commodities consist of about seventy-five pounds of food to last a month. Food full of preservatives, processed meats, canned food, white sugar,

Mad Bear

Wonder Bread, Jell-O, white flour.

Government figures it feeds an Indian for $37 a month. Diabetes is rampant in these tribal lands."

SOUTH DAKOTA STATE UNIVERSITY

RUSS:

"I've talked to people who have taught on the reservation and they'll tell you that the kids are dead by the eighth grade and they'll look at you and follow your instructions but we're not going anywhere. It's the old lights are on but the engines aren't running. We gotta stop that."

RUSSELL MEANS:

"Check your history books. We don't exist past the 1950s. There is no contemporary Native American history being taught today in schools."

PRAIRIE STAR GALLERY

CLINT:

"They're teaching Spanish to kindergarteners yet they don't have Native American studies in high school."

Plenty Wounds

RUSSELL MEANS:

"No wonder our People have such extreme low self-esteem. We don't exist. We're not important enough to be mentioned."

PHYLLIS:

"We have to create hope for our children."

WILL (teacher):

"Education is not one size fits all. These are little human beings we're working with. Little guys with souls and spirits. You have to treat them like human beings, not a bunch of little yankee doodle robots, they're little human beings!

To me, this is what 'no child left behind' is, is that you love every one of those children, have a vested interest in who they are, and have that desire to be a good teacher and to teach them all and to empower them.

I don't like seeing teachers gather with this lame philosophy of, 'If we've only saved one child then we've done our job.' From where I sit, if you've only saved one child, you should be terminated immediately, because you're lacking in teaching skills, you're lacking in people skills, you need to embrace all these children and do your job as a teacher."

Grey Hawk & Kills Crow

MAYOR'S OFFICE

MAYOR ALAN HANKS:

"How do I get the Native American community to get more involved? It's a struggle, they are very proud and private. Because of the nature of their culture and a perception that it doesn't make a difference. We've been struggling to get them to participate in the process."

KILI RADIO STATION PORCUPINE, SOUTH DAKOTA

CARS PARKED IN FRONT OF SMALL, FREE-STANDING BUILDING

NARRATOR:

"There are two radio stations on the Lakota reservations, KILI, owned and controlled by Lakota People. It plays traditional music, some programs in Lakota language and deals with things important to the Lakota.

And KILINI, owned and controlled by the Jesuits which bombards us with Catholicism.

Guess which radio station I listen to?"

KILI Radio Station

Lakota Disc Jockey, ARLO (20s) Speaks Into A Mic:

"I mentioned it before. Parents, it's your obligation to

Paul Brown Robe

go to parent/teacher conferences. Our Lady of Lourdes School, you have a conference at four p.m., so get over there."

BRAD PITT AND ANGELINA JOLIE AND THEIR ADOPTED KIDS

MADONNA AND HER ADOPTED FOREIGN KIDS

WILL:

"We're talking about human suffering here. Everybody that likes to go outside the country to adopt people. Don't you realize the same suffering is taking place within the borders of the United States? You know what? I'm not talking just about Indigenous People, I'm talking about poor little white kids too, I'm talking about poor little black kids, I'm talking about the poor little Hispanics, the little Asian kids. The way I talk, color has nothing to do with it. It has to do with the human state.

The greatness of a country should be measured on how well its children are taken care of and how well its women and its old folks are taken care of.

I think the only ones who really understand where I'm coming from are the old ones. They are great human beings. In Lakota society we don't throw them in an old folk's home or the equivalent of a pasture. We respect the integrity of being old and having that wisdom."

Thomas White Face

Traditional tribal music

IRENE'S HOUSE IN ROSEBUD

Irene sits at her table; her weathered face looks down in the traditional way for Lakota women. Cockroaches climb up the wall.

PRAIRIE STAR GALLERY

JOHN (40s):

"As a native artist, it's important to present us as contemporary Native Americans as opposed to the stereotyped Hollywood history.

Lone ranger on white horse and tonto on the brown pinto

That's all really good but not all there is. We're alive, we're not museum relics or a curiosity from a bygone age."

POW-WOW GROUNDS

Tribal music

Pine ridge

Will walks the circle beneath the four colors.

Eagle Woman that All Look At
the only woman recognized as a chief among the Sioux

WILL:

"Our women are strong, man! The backbone of the nation, they are who they say they are. Our men are kinda like wachinko a bit. Wachinko means pout. When you question their masculinity they just pout and they want to attack you, man. There's a few good men around, man.

Me and the guys I know we're like the Marines. We're looking for a few good men. Strong men — stand-up men — make-a-difference men - to mentor to these young guys, man. You know, come together and unite behind what political force we do have, make the United States more accountable, make the federal government more accountable, things of that nature.

We don't have leaders in that structured world who are really going to dig down and do it. I know a few, I know a couple.

But they have the same problems I had, everybody else had. Anybody who stands up and puts themselves out there, because of where you're at, they will tear you down in a New York minute. You know. Even less than that. Because they don't understand you are standing for them.

I've seen so many good people, boom, just go down. I've been there too. And at the traditional thing, we don't have any of the so-called chiefs. Na-cha. Headsmen who motivate. Who truly live for the People, you know. Who lead the People by example?

Peter Iron Shell

We've got some who can put on war bonnets and walk around and look really good, just like they walked out of pages of a history book, but it's kind of self-serving kind of stuff you know, kind of like a glamorization."

RUSSELL MEANS:
"We ourselves don't allow role models. It's part of the colonization."

A REZ HOUSE

MADONNA:
"Colonization is a broad term. And what that means is real basic - it's destruction of the family unit. The men lose their status right away. They were to provide and protect. In this modern day they can't do either. The result is what we have today."

WILL:
"When you live in poverty, you have to survive. If that means selling drugs, it means selling drugs. If that means being a being a corrupt politician, that's what it is. If that means being a dirty cop, that means being a cowardly man, that all you do to live every day to keep under everybody's radar so you can keep your job. I understand all

Wild Horse

that. That's the side effects of colonization, forced assimilation, all that.

I understand that, but those elements are going to remain stagnant until we can learn to be like our ancestors and come together. And that's all I'm saying. Sometimes I don't know how else to say it, I understand that it hurts some people's feelings, they act like I stole their last piece of fry bread and kicked their puppy while I was doing it. It's not meant to do that.

How do you motivate People? I don't know the answers. I've been there, I've tried and the most I got for my efforts was death threats and people conspiring to keep me from working and all this and that.

I can forgive my own People because I know what poverty does to People. Don't accept it, I don't condone it, but I understand it.

I don't know who the next leader of our People is going to be, I don't. We are kinda hurting."

MAYOR'S OFFICE

MAYOR ALAN HANKS:
"Those that are driven to be successful have a tendency to be shunned by their own community. They move away."

Lone Wolf

WILL:

"I know a bunch of good men out there. And without fail, every time they put themselves out there to become a dynamic difference in the community, they are the ones that become attacked. Because of people's desire to protect the crumbs that fell off of Uncle Sam's table. And it's not much, so control of those few crumbs is very dire for people like that.

When you start to understand that these people control who gets a job. When these people can gather groups to run you off and this and that.

It's a damn sad state of affairs, when the stone cold and Indigenous Lakota People, the ones who pray for this planet, the ones who pray for the People are the very reason that we have sovereignty in the first place are the ones that're under constant social attack.

What's even sadder is that the system, the bigger system, has allied with people from within the tribe. It's very very effective, man.

But see the thing is, to talk like this gives people bad flashbacks of the seventies. Of the sixties. And they're going to be quick to label you - oh he's a radical. Cesar Chavez, he's a radical. John Lennon, he was a radical. Russell Means, radical. They put a label on you, you know. Crazy Horse. Radical. Hostile.

Without being a radical, nothing gets done, but it's the system who is very effective at fooling people."

Slow Bull

KIDS JUMP ON A TRAMPOLINE IN A FRONT YARD

WILL:

"Is it radical to want your children to eat, your women to be safe?"

TRIBAL MUSIC

DRY WITHERED PLANTS

REZ HOUSE

MADONNA:

"Most of us saw what was going on with civil rights movement and anti-war movement, we didn't have to put up with it. So I became part of the Red Power movement and American Indian Movement when it got started in 1968.

It just swept the country, Indian country. There were organizations that sprang up all over."

RUSSELL MEANS:

"The American Indian Movement was a vanguard and it was a vanguard for self-determination and once the Indians grasped that, hey, we can demand things in America…"

Leonard Peltier

MADONNA:

"We were radicals, we were militants, shoot, they even called us communists. I like the word activists. Though the years taught us to be skeptical and question authority. The issues related to everybody. We affected policy change and it didn't come from the top down. It came from the People. There is a constant ongoing struggle with federal bureaucracies."

NARRATOR:

Leonard Peltier, a Dakota activist and AIM member was arrested in 1977 and sentenced to two life sentences for the murder shooting of two FBI agents on Pine Ridge. Witnesses in the trial, later admitted to being coerced and threatened to give false testimony by the FBI. Leonard remains in prison for 44 years as an American Indian prisoner of war. Long as Leonard is in prison, none of us are free.

RUSSELL MEANS:

"I've demonstrated, I've gone to prison, I've gone to the hospital because I've been shot, stabbed and beaten into a coma, all trying to get this country to live up to its own laws.

I've been jailed countless times, on as little as traffic tickets, taken out of the airport in handcuffs because of some traffic ticket. I know what this country is capable of. Suffered five assassination attempts in a four-year period

Iron Thunder – Crow Eagle
Fool Thunder – Slow White Buffalo

in the 1970s, so I know, I'm well aware of the mean spirit that can run through the American government. It just goes on and on. So what's left for us but freedom and independence? AIM brought us a glimpse of it through armed struggle."

HAROLD:

"I don't know if they accomplished what they set out to do, but they did bring attention to the living conditions, so in that way it was positive."

RUN-DOWN GOVERNMENT HOUSING

A "PATRIOT'S HOUSE" WITH AMERICAN FLAGS

ARMY CORPS OF ENGINEERS' MAPS

A REZ HOUSE

MADONNA:

"Along came the sixties when the federal government built a series of dams along the Missouri and started flooding the shoreline of any tribes along the Missouri.

We spent a lot of time growing up along the river. So when it was gone, I didn't realize until later years why I was so angry and mad at the world. Where I grew up is

Henry Crow Dog

underwater and it still is.

So I just had that feeling of land-loss and especially if you're tied to the land. I had the feeling that I knew what my ancestors felt like."

DAM AT FORT RANDALL, SOUTH DAKOTA

PHYLLIS:

"When I was ten-years-old they flooded all the bottom lands here on Standing Rock, fifty-five thousand acres and that's the most prime land in the whole Missouri River Basin. My home was taken."

SINGING AND TRIBAL MUSIC

AGAY:

"I think I had the best childhood growing up because we were on horseback all the time and riding and just free."

They put us in cluster homes, it was an uprooting of our culture and our traditions."

PHYLLIS:

"It's the most patriotic times in our country that they've taken the most from us. It was during Kennedy's era, under President Kennedy's Administration more land taken from the Lakota than any time in history.

Indian country is not legally private property, it's trust and trust is an assumed-taking.

Chief He Dog

The government says, 'oh well', the president writes off a signature, 'oh well', that's not trust, we have a treaty relationship with the United States. We see them as that, now the United States has to recognize that. Going back to the taking that happened under President Kennedy, and Standing Rock has had the most timber of any tribe in this river basin. So, my struggle for the last twenty years has been to reclaim what was taken from us in terms of our homes that were destroyed."

A TEACHER, ARTIST SITS IN HER ROCKING CHAIR

TILDA:
"We just had our own little paradise I guess, I would call it now, because we don't have it anymore."

PHYLLIS:
"There was no plan, no pre-plan, there was no NEPA, the National Environmental Policy Act, there was no environmental laws that said you had to adhere to this in order to take their lands, we didn't have that, our lands were flooded in the night, our men were singing their death songs because they knew everyone was dying because our lands were being flooded, our homes."

IZZY:
"They say our ancestors sold that land. Where is the documentation?"

WHITE BULL

White Bull
(Thathanka Ska)

MADONNA:

"How does the government keep the Indian weak and squabbling around for crumbs? Federal Indian Policy."

MAYOR'S OFFICE

MAYOR ALAN HANKS:

"The solution has to come from within their communities. They need to identify how they're going to make improvements. We can't tell them what the solutions are. Until they identify and start moving in that direction, there's not much we can do."

KILI RADIO STATION

ARLO:

"We're basically the burden of the United States government."

We hear lakota language spoken

RUSSELL MEANS:

"We have developed a language that you cannot insult another human being or any living thing. It's a stretch. It's a respectful and humble language and provides a world

Buffalo Bull Ghost

view about everything being a strand in a spiderweb. You cut one strand and you cut the spiderweb. Patriarchy has cut the spiderweb. In our language, it's impossible to express anger. And if you don't have the word, you don't have the concept. I don't care what redneck out there thinks we were all savages because I know better."

PHYLLIS:

"It has been devastating, devastating in terms of the language because only 16% of Lakotas speak the language fluently. And that's critical because our language is probably the most expressive language in the world and it is an extremely spiritual language.

You know the word 'wakan' means holy. The word for child is 'wakanja'. It's a derivative of holy and child means Sacred Being. And if you interpret your language and your thought processes and you identify your child as a Sacred Being and treat your child as such, then that child will be loved and spoiled good and reared and raised and nurtured and loved and be a beautiful human being."

RUSSELL MEANS:

"Now we're on the cusp of losing our language. The average age of a fluent Lakota speaker is sixty-five.

Linguists have already ascertained we've lost it. I don't believe it."

Charles American Horse

TIPIZIWAN:

"Our language should be a priority."

RUSSELL MEANS:

"Once we lose that language, we lose it, we lose who we are. We're gonna lose that? Intolerable. Not while I'm alive! So when you have this kind of beauty from your language and your connectedness, you understand the web of life. You're part of it. You're not superior or inferior, you're part of an entire mosaic of life."

MADONNA:

"Our grandmother was bi-lingual. Everyone spoke Indian to each other but English to us. 'It's a white man's world and I don't want my grandchildren to be handicapped so they're going to speak English.'"

MENTAL HEALTH OFFICE

LYLE:

"They wouldn't let us speak our language. Once the language is spoken and learned, you don't lose it. I kept mine through all the assimilation tactics."

Black Elk

NARRATOR:

"There's a movement - the Freedom Delegation wants to break away from United States and form a new, separate country, the Lakota Nation and demand the sacred Black Hills returned to our People."

BLACK HILLS

SNOW-COVERED TREES SWAY

MAYOR'S OFFICE

MAYOR ALAN HANKS:

"They're a sovereign nation and it makes it very difficult but yet they want to always make sure, they're always demanding rights, so are you a sovereign nation or are you not?

You have to choose. It's a struggle. It's a decision they need to make.

What direction? If they want to integrate into the rest of South Dakota and the culture, do they want to integrate or not?

Not lose their heritage? Do you want to become part of a community, even though you keep your identity? They need to lay out the course for their own future."

BOWLING ALLEY

MARCY (non-native):

"I don't think anybody's ever touched on what the problem is... so segregated, Indians and Whites...it's a perpetuation from the government.

People say enough is enough, but you start taking back and it might be a problem.

The Whites get tired of it, so much handouts. When the Indians whine... sorry, when the Native Americans whine, it's like having your kid in a candy store. They grab a candy bar and you should say "no" but it's easier to let them have it. The government should've said 'enough is enough now, guys'."

PRAIRIE EDGE GALLERY

U.S. SENATOR TOM DASCHLE:

"You know we've got a long way to go to living up to the expectations of the treaties and the commitments made by our country to Indian country and I think we have a lot of work in public policy in that regard as well."

JAMES (non-native):

"Our government's been so generous to them. Native Americans had a reputation of stealing. Store owners would follow them around the shop, watch 'em like they're thieves..."

Kills in Timber

BOWLING ALLEY

ASA:
"Somebody robbed a store, 'oh he's an Indian...'"

JESSICA:
"Some adults are against Indians, we get money for nothing. Whites should be able to too."

NICOLE:
"The parents say they can't hang around with us because we're Indian."

HIGH SCHOOL GYMNASIUM

BASKETBALL PLAYERS

BILLY:
"Martin's like that. Straight up racist."

HEALTH SERVICES OFFICES

LYLE:
"He thought I was a thief, an Indian thief."

RUSSELL MEANS:
"There used to be cowboys riding around in their trucks with a gun in the back window. They'd see Indians, jump out and beat 'em up and drive away.

Little Dog
(I-Me-Tacco)

The Indians started hanging in packs. It prevented that from happening again. Now they get cat-calls. The racism on the plains is vicious. News reporters, veterans of the south, couldn't believe the racism here.

Mobridge high school kids got off scot free. That's the kind of stuff that goes on, very blatant racism."

MENTAL HEALTH OFFICE

LYLE:

"Racism is still here. I don't think it'll go away. That's why I live here in Kyle."

NARRATOR:

"The weak, inferior man adopts racism. He thinks that by making someone else inferior, he makes himself superior. But that's not how it goes."

SOUTH DAKOTA STATE UNIVERSITY

SDSU STUDENT:

"The relatives are jealous of them. They're like, you're betraying your family. They're called 'Apples' there. White on the inside but Native American on the outside."

LYLE:

"The Whites have superiority and are in power and use it."

Poor Elk

RUSSELL MEANS:

"Real racist books, you wouldn't believe what was taught in grade schools.

There's an air base, Ellsworth Air Force Base outside of Rapid City. Lot of blacks. My son about five years ago was hanging out with blacks; and whites in front of the blacks, would call him Prairie Nigger. What'd those black guys say? Nothing..."

LYLE:

"There are a few good White People out there, but there are just so few here."

WILL:

"We don't need anybody to oppress us anymore. I mean they've gotten us to the place where we do a fine job of doing that, thank you very much."

NARATOR:

"Lakota are real good at grudges both tribal, inter-tribal: Crow Dog and Spotted Tail, Blackfeet, the White Men, Crow, Mexicans, Pawnee, Ojibway, traditionalists and the Catholics, half-breeds and full-bloods, peyote people. We hold onto our grudges, we never forget."

Chief
No Flesh
of the Sioux

No Flesh

MAYOR'S OFFICE

MAYOR ALAN HANKS:

"There's probably racism everywhere in the world. It's just human nature. I want to continue to work on it but I don't think you can solve racism. It will be part of society forever. Racism goes every single direction.

There's racism against Native Americans but it's also there for tall guys with beards."

WILL:

"Justice, what is justice, man? All I know is that it doesn't exist for us in this world. The only place where justice probably becomes a reality for us, the only form of justice is spiritual justice.

You know, when the Creator comes back to say, all right that's enough of you people, man. This is the way it is. We ain't gonna find it in the courtrooms. We're not gonna find it in the halls of congress. Those words on the Declaration of Independence, the Constitution, the Bill of Rights - we should be making those words come to life instead of just empty rhetoric sitting on a page somewhere.

So I see so many good people out there who are trying.

All we can do is, man, when they feel down is just to encourage them. And pray for them."

Iron Hawk (Chetan Maza)

LAKOTA FACES

NARRATOR:

"Loss of culture - loss of language - suicide - jail - alcoholism - drugs - diabetes - disrespect - intertribal hostility - poor nutrition - poor health care - poor education. Despair. Defeat. Anger. Deep depression. Indians want to go back in history. Go back before the White Man, but they can't.

The White Man can say to us 'hey get over it, what's past is past' - but for most of us the depression won't go away, just like racism doesn't go away, it is passed on from generation to generation also.

We just can't pretend the past didn't happen, that it doesn't exist today."

SOUTH DAKOTA STATE UNIVERSITY

RUSS:

"How do we change it? Because it requires a systematic change, not a short time cure, but a systemic change."

Eagle Man

THE BADLANDS

NARRATOR:

"For more than fifty years our People have been exposed to radioactive pollution from abandoned open pit uranium mines, toxic waste dump sites, and hidden underground US Air Force nuclear power plants in remote areas on the reservations.

President Nixon signed a secret Executive Order declaring this region a "National Sacrifice Area" for mining and production of uranium and nuclear energy. Same exact area the 1868 Ft Laramie Treaty gave to the Great Sioux Nation.

Run-off from open pit uranium mines has polluted the Cheyenne River and aquifers that bring drinking water to Pine Ridge Reservation. In some samples radiation levels found to be 120,000 times above safe normal levels.

Levels of arsenic, uranium in drinking water found in Pine Ridge up to 12 times higher than the safe levels told to us by the Clean Drinking Water Act. Lakota are dying from cancer at a 30% greater rate than White Men in South Dakota.

Diabetes at a rate eight times greater than the rest of the nation, our children are born with downs and alcohol syndrome. Deformities. The rate of infant mortality is five times greater than the national average.

Black Thunder

Indian Health Service installed arsenic filters on drinking water coming into homes on Pine Ridge.

Some of the old water wells have been capped. Water now comes from the river, by pipeline. But this pipeline does not reach remote areas of the reservation that still depend on groundwater for drinking water.

The U.S. government must put an end to future uranium mining and dumping their wastes on our sacred lands and continue to clean up the uranium and arsenic mess! But we all know they won't"

IZZY:

"We don't have a religion like the White Man. It's just you and the Creator. If you do that, you live a good life. There's almost no red road anymore. Literally, we're trying to rebuild a nation, bring back what was taken from us... we didn't lose our way, we're just out here wandering around."

NARRATOR:

"So why do the People stay on the reservation if conditions are so bad you might ask?"

Gray Eagle

AN OLD GRIZZLED CEDAR TREE

IZZY:

"In the beginning, before anybody was here, the Creator put a big giant cedar tree on a hill and told the tree, 'I want you watch over things for me. I have other things I must attend to.'

Thousands of years later Creator came back. 'How are you doing Grandson?'

I'm all right' answered the tree.

'How was it?'

'Wakan Tanka, I did everything you asked of me. I stood in the hottest of hot, coldest of cold. The hardest part was, I was lonely.'

'That's good, Grandson. For what you did for me, I'm now going to give you all your relatives.' And the tree looked around and suddenly he was surrounded by other trees. As far as he could see, there was a forest.

And in the same way, the Lakota believe they're supposed to live that way, surrounded by family. That's why they stay."

MADONNA:

"Colonized people are going to hang onto that federal umbilical cord until the Feds cut it. And they're not going to cut it, they're going to stop the money little by little. So

White Belly

they don't have to get rid of the Indian problem, they'll just defund everything."

MOUNTAIN TOP

JAMES:

"See through the eyes of your heart and you'll see the truth. We're suffering, we're burning up. The rains don't come, it's almost over..."

IRENE'S HOUSE AT ROSEBUD

IRENE:

"I'm sitting here showing you my ugly house, hoping it'll help my People."

Soft traditional tribal music and drumming

Prairie

The sun rises over the badlands

WILL:

"I don't mind living with things, but the women and children shouldn't have to. And it's that very element of being a man... a lot of our men, a lot of them won't say nothing you know.

That's how we've become conditioned to poverty and unbalanced scales. There used to be a time when we would come together and I tried. But I don't think they care now, man."

Crazy Bear

PHYLLIS:

"We're done surviving, we want to thrive."

WILL:

"You cannot separate yourself or let that ego get carried away. (speaks Lakota) 'I'm just a common man.' No matter what I do in this life it's important for me not to lose that connection with the poorest of the poor. Because I never know when I'm going to become that too. So, you have to stay grounded. Anything that's done successfully is not gonna be one by one or two.

One or two is an easy target. You have to do it together. We have to talk with each other with compassion. That's the responsibility of us so-called adults. If we can't do that, we've failed, that and handing them down a planet that can never be fixed.

The last time our people banded together was when they fought Custer. It wasn't only the Dakota, Nakota and Lakota. It was the Shoshone, the Arapaho and Cheyenne.

And that was a big thing back then for everybody to come together for one purpose.

If we took that much effort today for one purpose, I think a lot more would get done.

If we want things to happen, we've got to get together, band together and do it. Not in the aspect of for myself or my generation but for generations yet to come. How are they supposed to learn if they don't see us doing it?"

Big Road

BILL:

"A lot of them on the rez have given up a long time ago trying to fight for it. I don't know the answers but I try to be a friend to all of them."

MAYOR'S OFFICE

MAYOR ALAN HANKS:

"We need to make sure we maintain a prosperous community - economic development. The struggle for us has always been how to create good paying jobs so people can move back here.

The biggest asset we have as a community is the beauty of the area, whether it's the black hills, the badlands or the prairie."

MADONNA:

"If it wasn't for the land base, we'd be treated like the rest of the poor people in this country. The American way of greed. Because we have a land base, there are remnants of tribal ways."

His Hoop

MAYOR'S OFFICE

MAYOR ALAN HANKS:

"You have to make them understand if they stay in school, there is a better future for them. For some reason there is a perception that because they're Native American they don't have those opportunities."

PINE RIDGE POW-WOW GROUNDS

WILL:

"Please grow up. Have a little bit of maturity.

'With education comes the job?'- Really?

You can't find a job here with 85% unemployment rate, because we don't have an established economic infrastructure. All of our money goes off to support infrastructures around us, like in the towns of Chadron and Rapid City.

You know what? Those who say we're getting free handouts and all that? I think Walmart and all those guys would be very upset at you for attacking us because that's where we take our money. They're the ones that benefit."

LYLE:

"We need more jobs here. Our college graduates students every June and there aren't enough jobs to go around."

Fool Bull

HIGHER GROUNDS COFFEE SHOP

LEON:

"Men get discouraged because there are no jobs here, teens look at it and lose hope, kill themselves..."

LAKOTA TEENS

PHYLLIS:

"One thing that was unanimous was that all the young people wanted to leave."

MAYOR ALAN HANKS:

"In essence, we almost have a brain drain here. Those folks who have the ability to excel, they want to move out and find opportunities. We need to create those opportunities."

IZZY:

"We're in pretty rough shape all over the world. They have to stop destroying the earth, the air, the water."

FACTORIES SPEW POISONOUS BLACK SMOKE

MADONNA:

"The Old People said, 'Mother earth is going to clean up and if the humans gotta go, they gotta go.' I'm all for that"

One Bull

SOUTH DAKOTA STATE UNIVERSITY

BOB:

"Who are my People?

When I was an aircraft commander it was everyone on that airplane. Take care of them.

When I was a squadron commander it was the people in my squadron.

When I was a pastor it was the people in the community I served.

And here who are my People?

Why are the People in need not my neighbors? I can do something about that. It's a philosophy about if I can't make something better then what's the purpose of being here? I believe that the world is my community. There are no bounds to my community."

MAYOR ALAN HANKS:

"We're all immigrants, with the exception of the Native Americans. We've all come from different parts of the world and we've all found the way to integrate yet keep our identity."

MADONNA:

"Fear is part of being human. So, what are you going to do about it? That's what takes courage."

Three Bears

WILL:

"They say, 'America love it or leave it.' We say, 'America, love it or give it back.'"

RUSSELL MEANS:

"I'm sixty-nine winters old and don't want to fight anymore."

PHYLLIS:

"This is our homeland, we have nowhere else to go. We have no gene pool anywhere else in the world. This is our home. This is where we are, where we must be, we must defend, we must live and die here. We have to create our own economies, we have to initiate, anything that we want to do for our own People we have to do it ourselves."

WILL:

"Around here you, if you don't condition yourself to be strong and look at the positive side of things, you're in for a hell of a ride, man, you're in for a downward spiral. You have to always keep that hope alive!"

MADONNA:

"We all do what we can in our lifetime. We're all human, there are no superheroes. We just do what we can do to help our People."

Yellow Shirt

WILL:

"As long as the language is there, there's still hope and just, never quit. Never ever quit. And in the end if all you've managed to do is empower someone to have that same kind of don't ever quit attitude, then it's cool, it's cool."

PHYLLIS:

"We are a very unique People. We still have our land base. We have our culture. We have our language. We still have all the criteria that makes us a nation. May be broken and battered, but we still have it.

We have to rebuild what we have and I believe that we have enough Lakota People that are gifted, talented and strong, both men and women and we have enough room in our struggle for everyone to partake in it."

KILI RADIO STATION

DEREK:

"There's a lot of smart people out there, our natives got a lot of talent, they can do anything, anything they want."

Red Wing

MADONNA:

"We still have our identity."

PHYLLIS:

"Hope to live. Not to survive. We're done surviving. We're done digging our fingers through pain to live.

And where we want to live. We want to thrive in a good way and we want to have a positive life style. So that's what this is about."

SOUTH DAKOTA STATE UNIVERSITY

BOB:

"I've been in enough societies to know that we're not different, we're all the same people."

SDSU STUDENT:

"We have to realize we all have to team up and get something happening."

NARRATOR:

"The big battle that the Lakota fight today is the right to clean water. To stop the Dakota Access Pipeline from crossing and polluting eight hundred miles of Lakota treaty and sacred land. Mni wichoni, water is not only for life, water is life, water is sacred.

Lakota warriors lead a battle against Big Oil, government contractors and corporate greed at Standing Rock

169

Water Warriors

Reservation, Rosebud and Cheyenne River Reservations to stop the Keystone XL Pipeline from building their pipeline under the Cheyenne and Missouri Rivers, the main sources of tribal water. A leak or spill would poison drinking water of ten million People.

The black thirty-inch pipe, one thousand, one hundred and seventy-two miles long is warned about in our Ancient One's Prophecy that a big black snake will come to us one day to destroy our world unless the Youth, our Children stop it.

In response states are criminalizing pipeline protesters.

In recent water protests on Standing Rock, the National Guard watched as security contractors turned attack dogs on peaceful protesters.

Grandmothers, Oglala elders and teens on horses were teargassed, tased, arrested while rubber bullets were shot into the protesters.

This present protest is called NoDAPL, the goal is to leave a clean and healthy environment for seven future generations.

LAKOTA SPIRITUAL ACTIVIST CHERYL ANGEL (from the Esperanza Project interview with Tracy L Barnett):

"We all know what to do. Stand Up Fight Back! But to do it in a way that our ancestors would be proud of us.

Eagle Dog

Our ancestors never went looking for a fight. We are defenders of the People; we are not troublemakers. We were taught how to recognize nature as a powerful, living source that we treated with respect; that's where the animals lived; that's where we got our sustenance, that's where we set up temporary homes – we were so careful not to leave a trace, that the next year we had to find the landmarks we left to remember where we camped – because there were times we buried our dead along the trail and left landmarks for them. Our relationship with the land is everything. How we live on those lands is everything we need to know. We were taught to live in peace.

I've always carried the old ways inside, the words of my grandmothers – I was raised to always do the right thing for others – and even if I was reluctant, because I was the only one doing it, my grandma would say: 'Especially if you're the only one who is doing the right thing, then you have to, or nobody will see what they should be doing.'

What's so radical about opening our lands to the buffalo and taking down the fences and letting the water run free and clean?

Without their (water protester's) honest reporting as to the impact of these oil and gas and fracking pipelines to water, the people who will be affected won't know the truth of how devastating pipelines are to watersheds and rivers and their water supply.

Right now, we're just pebbles. But when we march

Arthur Iron Nest

together, and we sit down and pray – we're a rock.

Humanity has left a damaging legacy that is changing our climate and we must stop using fossil fuels and move forward with renewable energies and focus on supporting sustainable economies in our lives."

MISSING AND MURDERED INDIGENOUS WOMEN AND GIRLS HUMAN RIGHTS CRISIS

NARRATOR:

"The People fight another battle today. The battle to prevent the murder of and to find missing indigenous women and girls.

Nearly six thousand missing and murdered Indigenous Women and Girls each year plague our Indigenous People.

This crime is felt by all Native People, families and communities. The crime is ten times greater than the national average.

Black Coyote

White system of justice has failed us.

We must try harder to protect our sacred women who bring beauty, love and life.

PLEASE NO MORE STOLEN SISTERS!

PRAIRIE EDGE GALLERY

TOM DASCHLE:
"Well, what they didn't know is that it is still a land rich in resources. Wind resources and sun resources."

WINDMILLS SPIN

RUSSELL MEANS:
"The great Mystery has blessed my country with the finest wind in the contiguous 48 states. We have sun 340 days of the year, sun power. We have geothermal water out of our holy land, the Black Hills. Aquaculture, solar power, green houses."

MADONNA:
"It's a ray of hope for everybody."

Many Horses

PRAIRIE EDGE GALLERY

TOM DASCHLE:
"So, I believe that alternative energy development as we go into the climate change will be a real Godsend in Indian country and we're working on that now."

PHYLLIS:
"I have real hope."

RUSSELL MEANS:
"We have to include White People and everything we treasure will come back to us. All the sacred colors of the human race deserve themselves. We can't change that; we don't have that right. So, we want to include them again in our vision."

NARRATOR:
"Many Horses an Oglala Medicine Man friend of Sitting Bull organized the Ghost Dance at Standing Rock in 1890 to dance away the white soldiers camped nearby, but in the morning the soldiers were still camped there, Great Spirit spoke to him."

MANY HORSES:
"I will follow the whiteman's trail. I will make him my friend, but I will not bend my back to his burdens. I will

Whirling Horse

be cunning as a coyote. I will ask him to help me understand his ways, then I will prepare the way for my children, and their children. The Great Spirit has shown me – a day will come when we will outrun the white man in his own shoes."

PICTURESQUE LANDSCAPE

DEREK:

"A lot of people say it's all bad and this and that, but me personally I love it, it's like home and there's no other place like it. Our People have always lived with struggle. That's what makes us so strong."

FIELDS OF WILDFLOWER

GIANT CEDAR TREE AT SYLVAN LAKE

JOHN:

"We're alive. Our women are doctors, they're lawyers, they're truckers. Our men are doing good things, we're thriving. We're not gone, we weren't killed off, we're doing great things."

RESTORATION BY
GARY COFFRIN

Strikes With Nose

GYMNASIUM

A WINTER POW-WOW

CHILDREN IN BRIGHTLY-COLORED TRADITIONAL OUTFITS
DANCE IN A CIRCLE

THEIR FACES GLOW WITH PRIDE

PHYLLIS:

"I'm a mother, I'm a grandmother. I'm a patriot to my own People. I have to create life. That's my duty as a mother and a grandmother to create life, to make life and to make life better."

SOUTH DAKOTA STATE UNIVERSITY

RUSS:

"To see people making it, having a good life, healthy. That's your reward. You don't get more.

Let's all pull the wagon together and we can move it out of the mud."

PINE RIDGE

NARRATOR:

"Help is on the way. It is not coming from the government. It is coming from the Lakota People. Up to recent, only jobs on the reservation were through Bureau

Kicks the Iron

of Indian Affairs, casinos, and tourism, tribal offices and the Tribal Police office.

But a new breed of industries is popping up on the reservation.

For years big American Corporations have sent American jobs overseas. Outsourcing billions of dollars to India and Pakistan.

Recently these same corporations, frustrated by language problems that come with foreign outsourcing are now sending work to the Lakota Reservations.

In an attempt to preserve and restore Lakota culture, Russell Means began work on the T.R.E.A.T.Y. Emersion School. Patterned after successful Indigenous Language Immersion Schools of New Zealand for the Maori tribes.

Russell's school teaches tribal children Lakota language and restores Lakota identity to the young.

HOSPITAL

DOCTORS AND NURSES
Doctors and scientists are working on reversal of the diabetic epidemic and programs to teach the Lakota families about nutrition.

SOLAR FARMS AND WINDMILLS
The world is turning its focus to alternative energy – wind, solar and geothermal. Department of Energy estimates

Fire Lightning

native lands could produce 22% of energy demands of the country through renewable energy.

KILI RADIO STATION WINDMILL

In 2008 KILI radio station in Porcupine, South Dakota on the Pine Ridge Reservation installed a single wind turbine to generate all power to run the station, saving an estimated $12,000 in yearly energy costs. The only wind powered radio station in America.

WIND TURBINE FARMS

There are plans to build huge wind turbine farms across Lakota lands.

PINE RIDGE

ABANDONED CARS LITTER THE STREETS

TEEN GANG MEMBERS WALK IN GROUPS

DRUG DEALS

The Robert Wood Johnson Foundation gave Sinta Gleska University a $250,000 annual grant to establish drug and alcohol abuse treatment services for Lakota youth in trouble with the law and promote cultural tradition and horsemanship, spiritual knowledge, archery and traditional dancing to restore youth cultural identity.

Chief Two Strike

PINE RIDGE

Companies such as Lakota Express employ native college graduates who otherwise would have left the reservation in search of work.

Information technology, records management, help desk, and call centers are now set up on the reservations.

Lakota Express is working on a contract to supply buffalo meat to China.

COLLEGES AND MUSEUMS

Six colleges are now built on Lakota reservations: Oglala Lakota College, Si Tanka University, Sinte Gleska University, Sitting Bull College, Sisseton Wahpeton Community, Lower Brule Community College, and five museums to preserve Lakota culture.

A virtual high school set up in Shannon County so that young people can continue education on their own time. There are scholarships available to tribal members for college.

PINE RIDGE CONVENIENCE STORE AND GAS STATION

A new "SHOP LOCAL" campaign began to encourage tribal members to spend their money locally. Not only good for local business, but the 4% sales tax is returned to the reservation by the state, over 1.2 million dollars to help with social services.

189

Goose Face

Tribal members are encouraged to fill their gas tanks on the rez now because the .02% gas tax, that's around one million dollars a year is returned to the rez for road improvements, creating funds for training and long-term employment.

SUBWAY STORE

A new locally owned Subway store opened up on Pine Ridge and two new stores are going to open, employing over 30 Indians.

OUT OF BOUNDS BURGERS

Locally owned in Pine Ridge.

LAKOTA LOANS

Operated by Pine Ridge tribal members. lent out over $4,000,000 to over 331 businesses, artists and contractors and helped to create over 947 jobs.

BADLANDS

SOFT DRUMMING

There is now a moratorium on mining on sacred Lakota lands. And for now construction of the pipeline is temporarily halted.

High Hawk. ● Little Wound. ● Big Road
Two Strike. ● Fire Lightning. ● Afraid of his Horses
Spotted Elk

1891 Sioux Delegation to Washington DC

after Wounded Knee

LAKOTA TRIBAL CEREMONIAL MUSIC

GOOGLE EARTH: THE CONTINENT OF NORTH AMERICA SPINS SLOWLY

WE CAN MAKE OUT MOUNTAINS, SPARKLING LAKES AND RIVERS

PRAIRIE AND CHECKERED FARMLANDS

Yes, we have been lying down for a long time. But we are a nation of warriors and hunters, we will not let our People die. We are still alive. We are starting to get up now. Starting to taste life again. To taste freedom. And find and claim our spirit and our souls again."

TRIBAL MUSIC

WILD MUSTANGS

EAGLES

HERDS OF WILD BUFFALO ROAM THE VAST IMMUTABLE PRAIRIE

I wish to humbly thank:

Robin Bradford and Brightline Film Crew

Phyllis Young

Trish Burke, Community Outreach Director,
  Native Hope

Sheri Lohr, editor & book designer, SeaStory Press

Michele Taube for beta reading

Capt John Barrett Yates for proof reading and editing

Cody Taube for cover design

Will Peters

Sitting Bull

Flying Hawk

Webster Two Hawk

Leon Matthews

Harrold Thompsen

Madonna Thunder Hawk

Rae Ann Red Owl

Lyle Noisy Hawk

KILI Radio

Irene

James Shot-With-Two-Arrows

Agay Kingman

Russell Means

Alan Hanks

Tom Daschle

Mark St Pierre

Russell Stubbles

Clint Cottonwood

Arlo Ironcloud

Lisa

Marcy

Mike

Art

Bill Groethe

James Shirtzinger

Deb

John

Cheryl Angel

Crazy Horse

Many Horses

The Lakota Nation

And Izzy Zephier – (voice of the Narrator)

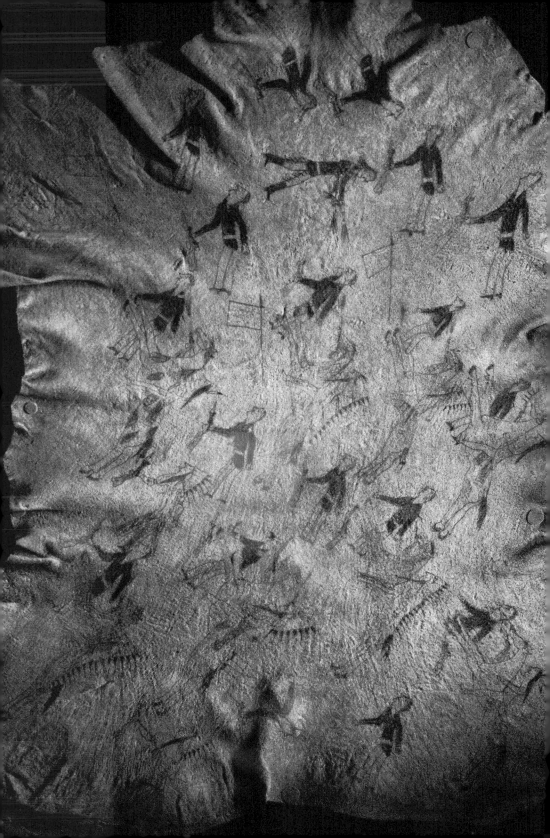

Printed in Great Britain
by Amazon